D0441089

The Six
Brandenburg Concertos

BWV 1046–1051

From the Bach-Gesellschaft Edition

Johann Sebastian Bach

DOVER PUBLICATIONS, INC.
Mineola, New York

Copyright

Copyright © 1997 by Dover Publications, Inc.
Preface copyright © 1976 by Dover Publications, Inc.
All rights reserved.

Bibliographical Note

This Dover edition, first published in 1997, is a republication of music from "Joh. Seb. Bach's Kammermusik. Dritter Band" [1871], edited by Wilhelm Rust, in *Johann Sebastian Bach's Werke*, originally published by the Bach-Gesellschaft in Leipzig.

The quotation on page ix is from Albert Schweitzer's *J. S. Bach, le musicien-poète*, 1905, translated by Ernest Newman.

International Standard Book Number

ISBN-13: 978-0-486-29795-8
ISBN-10: 0-486-29795-0

Manufactured in the United States by LSC Communications
29795011   2018
www.doverpublications.com

CONTENTS

BWV numbers refer to Wolfgang Schmieder's *Bach-Werke-Verzeichnis*
[Catalog of Bach's Works], the standard systematic-thematic reference work
for the music of Johann Sebastian Bach.

To Christian Ludwig, Margrave of Brandenburg

THE SIX BRANDENBURG CONCERTOS
(Cöthen and Weimar, 1711–1720)

Preface

Bach himself intended these concertos as a set. The basic source for the edition was the well-preserved autograph MS score, which once belonged to Johann Philipp Kirnberger, and later to his pupil Princess Amalie, sister of Frederick the Great; she bequeathed it to the Berlin *gymnasium* "Joachimsthal." The original parts of No. 5 are in the Berlin Royal Library.

The original title reads: "Six Concerts Avec plusieurs Instruments Dédiées A Son Altesse Royalle Monseigneur Crêtien Louis, Marggraf de Brandenbourg etc. etc. par Son tres-humble et tres obeissant serviteur Jean Sebastien Bach. Maitre de Chapelle de S. A. S. le prince regnant d'Anhalt-Coethen" (Six concertos with several instruments, dedicated to His Royal Highness Christian Ludwig, Margrave of Brandenburg, etc., by his very humble and obedient servant Johann Sebastian Bach, orchestral conductor of His Most Serene Highness the reigning Prince of Anhalt-Cöthen).

The original dedication reads: "A Son Altesse Royalle Monseigneur Crêtien Louis Marggraf de Brandenbourg &c. &c. &c. Monseigneur. Comme j'eus il y a une couple d'années, le bonheur de me faire entendre à Votre Altesse Royalle, en vertu de ses ordres, & que je remarquai alors, qu'Elle prennoit quelque plaisir aux petits talents que le Ciel m' a donnés pour la Musique, & qu' en prennant Conge de Votre Altesse Royalle, Elle voulut bien me faire l'honneur de me commander de Lui envoyer quelques pieces de ma Composition: j'ai donc selon ses tres gracieux ordres, pris la liberté de rendre mes tres-humbles devoirs à Votre Altesse Royalle, par les presents Concerts, que j'ai accommodés à plusieurs Instruments; La priant tres-humblement de ne vouloir pas juger leur imperfection, à la rigueur du gout fin et delicat, que tout le monde sçait qu'Elle a pour les piéces musicales; mais de tirer plutot en benigne Consideration, le profond respect, & la tres-humble obéissance que je tache à Lui temoigner par là. Pour le reste, Monseigneur, je supplie tres humblement Votre Altesse Royalle, d'avoir la bonté de continüer ses bonnes graces envers moi, et d'être persuadèe que je n'ai rien tant à coeur, que de pouvoir être employé en des occasions plus dignes d'Elle et de son service, moi qui suis avec un zele sans pareil / Monseigneur / De Votre Altesse Royalle / Le tres humble & tres obeissant serviteur / Jean Sebastien Bach. Coethen. d. 24 Mar. [Mai?] 1721" (To His Royal Highness Christian Ludwig, Margrave of Brandenburg, etc. Sire: Since I had the happiness, a few years ago, to play by command before Your Royal Highness, and observed at that time that you derived some pleasure from the small musical talent that Heaven has given me; and since, when I was taking leave of Your Royal Highness, you did me the honor to request that I send you some of my compositions: I have therefore, in compliance with your most gracious demand, taken the liberty of tendering my most humble respects to Your Royal Highness with the present concertos, arranged for several instruments, begging you most humbly not to judge their imperfection by the strict measure of the refined and delicate taste in musical pieces that everyone knows you possess, but rather to consider kindly the deep respect and the most humble obedience which I am thereby attempting to show to you. For the rest, Sire, I beseech Your Royal Highness most humbly to have the kindness to preserve your good will toward me and to be convinced that I have nothing so much at heart as to be able to be employed on occasions more worthy of you and your service, since I am with matchless zeal, Sire, Your Royal Highness' most humble and obedient servant, Johann Sebastian Bach. Cöthen, March [May?] 24, 1721).

Though the Brandenburg Concertos are a set by force of their 1721 date and dedication, they differ in genre and trend, and probably were composed at various times. Nos. 1 and 3 are more truly orchestral in style, and Bach later used their opening movements as symphonic introductions to cantatas (respectively, No. 52, "Falsche Welt, dir trau ich nicht," and No. 174, "Ich liebe den Höchsten von ganzem Gemüthe"). No. 5 is actually a clavier concerto, No. 4 a violin concerto. No. 2 has four solo instruments with equal roles, whereas No. 6 is in "quartet" style.

The first edition of these concertos was published by C. F. Peters of Leipzig in 1850.

CONCERTO NO. 1: The heading in the autograph MS reads: "Concerto 1mo à 2 Corni di Caccia, 3 Hautb: è Bassono, Violino Piccolo concertato, 2 Violini, una Viola è Violoncello, col Basso Continuo."

Page 8, m. 8: The second note in the Continuo is a-flat in the MS; altered here on the basis of the parallel passage (page 5, m. 3) and the cantata in which this movement was reused.

Page 13, m. 9: The MS has a natural sign before the fourth note of the Violino Piccolo; altered here on the basis of the Oboe part, page 12, m. 8.

CONCERTO NO. 2: The MS heading reads: "Concerto 2do à 1 Tromba, 1 Fiauto, 1 Hautbois, 1 Violino concertati, è 2 Violini, 1 Viola è Violone in Ripieno col Violoncello è Basso per il Cembalo." The MS has a G-clef for the flute; this was characteristic of recorder notation.

Page 34, m. 2: In the MS, the solo Flute, Oboe and Violin have d as the fourteenth 16th-note, while the Violins of the ripieno have f. But on page 29, m. 3, they all have f.

Page 50, mm. 9 & 10: The MS gives a-flat in the solo voices, a in the ripieno.

CONCERTO NO. 3: The MS heading reads: "Concerto 3to a tre Violini, tre Viole, è tre Violoncelli col Basso per il Cembalo."

Page 67, m. 4: In the MS the third note in Violin II is e, which creates an octave with Viola I.

Page 76, m. 1: In the MS the eighth 8th-beat in Violin II is d.

CONCERTO NO. 4: The MS heading reads: "Concerto 4to à Violino Principale, due Fiauti d'Echo, due Violini, una Viola è Violone in Ripieno, Violoncello è Continuo."

This is certainly a violin concerto, as proven, for example, by the figures in the last measures on page 77, the double stopping on page 88 and the use of the open E and A strings on pages 108 & 109. Bach reworked this as an F Major clavier concerto.

Page 80, m. 10: In the MS Flute II had a as the fourth and fifth notes; this did not correspond to any of the parallel passages.

CONCERTO NO. 5: The MS heading reads: "Concerto 5to â une Traversiere, une Violino principale, une Violino è una Viola in ripieno, Violoncello, Violone è Cembalo concertato." The editor of the 1850 Peters first edition preferred the MS parts to the MS score when readings diverged; usually parts are to be preferred, as coming later and embodying improvements, but in this case the autograph MS score is a very clean and neat later copy. The dynamic marks are fuller and more accurate in the score; another factor showing that the MS score we possess is later than the MS parts is a correction in it made by Bach: attempting to avoid parallel octaves with the solo Violin, he changed one bar of the Viola line (page 117, m. 11 of this volume) to read

Since, however, this is even worse, creating fifths

with the Clavier, the first form of the passage has been adopted here. Passages where the MS score has here been preferred to the MS parts are as follows:

Page 121, m. 4: page 126, mm. 2 & 5; and page 144, mm. 16–18: In the parts the Violone has full-measure rests.

Page 131, m. 6; page 132, m. 7; and page 133, mm. 1 & 5: In the parts the 32nd-note figure does not occur, and there are merely 16th-notes.

Page 134, mm. 6–12: In the parts the low *a* is marked to be held throughout.

Page 149, mm. 10–13 are missing in the parts, where after m. 9 the passage resumes:

CONCERTO NO. 6: The MS heading reads: "Concerto 6to à due Viole da Braccio, due Viole da Gamba, Violoncello, Violone e Cembalo."

Page 158, m. 3: In the MS, Viola I has *e* instead of *e*-flat, and Viola da Gamba I has for the second half of the measure.

The Six
Brandenburg Concertos

BWV 1046–1051

The Brandenburg concertos are the purest products of Bach's polyphonic style. Neither on the organ nor on the clavier could he have worked out the architecture of a movement with such vitality; the orchestra alone permits him absolute freedom in the leading and grouping of the obbligato voices . . . It is not now a question merely of the alternation of the *tutti* and the *concertino;* the various tone-groups interpenetrate and react on each other, separate from each other, unite again, and all with an incomprehensible artistic inevitability.

Albert Schweitzer

Brandenburg Concerto No. 1 in F Major

Menuetto.

Fine.

Menuetto da Capo, e poi il Trio.

Menuetto da Capo sino alla Fine.

Brandenburg Concerto No. 2 in F Major

Brandenburg Concerto No. 3 in G Major

Brandenburg Concerto No. 4 in G Major

Brandenburg Concerto No. 5 in D Major

Cembalo solo senza stromenti.

Brandenburg Concerto No. 6 in B-flat Major

Adagio ma non tanto.

Allegro.

END OF EDITION